Words like a river

Words like a river

A collection of lyrics and poems

Favor U

iUniverse, Inc.
Bloomington

Words like a river
A collection of lyrics and poems

iUniverse books may be ordered through booksellers or by contacting:

iUniverse
1663 Liberty Drive
Bloomington, IN 47403
www.iuniverse.com
1-800-Authors (1-800-288-4677)

ISBN: 978-1-4620-2359-2 (sc)
ISBN: 978-1-4620-2360-8 (ebk)

Printed in the United States of America

iUniverse rev. date: 05/19/2011

Contents

POEMS

Dedication

I dedicate this piece of work to the lovers of music.

Prologue

The feeling that breaks my heart and mends my heart again

The word that joins together without a string

Its powerful without measure, it melts even the heart of warriors

That word is L O V E

It lives in me . . . . , Abides in you

LYRICS

Please come back

Intro

Bell sound giggles
Hmm . . . . hmmm
In my mind it giggles
(yeah, yeah, yeah, yeah)
Baby is time for us to face the truth
Huh . . . . huhhhh . . . . huh

Verse 1

I can't imagine that you are gone
Of all the things that we went through
Even the words that you whispered
You've made them untrue

(Pre-Chorus)

Please come back baby
I really want you back
I know they hurt you bad,
We can make it again

Chorus

By our side we vowed, we will make it
By the bond of love we will be (together)
By the love we share we will fight
By our love we will conquer

By our sides we vowed, oh baby we did
By the bond of love we will be (yeah we will be)
By the love we share we will fight
By our love will conquer yeah we will

Verse 2

Please put your mind to the past memories and all we shared together
You know I love you no matter what I'm ready to fight for you
No matter what would strive I was always by your side
Be assured, oh . . . baby . . . . I need you back

Pre-Chorus

Please come back baby
I really want you back
I know they hurt you bad
Please come back

Chorus

By our side we vowed, we will make it
By the bond of love we will be (hmm . . . together)
By the love we share we will fight
By our love we will conquer
By our sides we vowed, oh baby we did
By the bond of love we will be (yeah we will be)
By the love we share we will fight
By our love will conquer yeah we will

Bridge

By the river side we stood
By the bond of love we vowed we will be,
By our strength of love we will conquered,
By our story we shall be remembered.
By our side we vowed, we will make it
By the bond of love we will be (together)
By the love we share we will fight
By our love we will conquer
By our sides we vowed, oh baby we did
By the bond of love we will be (yeah we will be)
By the love we share we will fight
By our love will conquer yeah we will

Outro

By our side we vowed we will make it (yeah together)
By the bond of love we will be (yeah together)
By the love we share we will fight
By our love we will conquer (hmm . . . together)
By our sides we vowed, oh baby we did
By the bond of love we will be (yeah we will be)
By the love we share we will fight
By our love will conquer yeah we will

(Chorus continues till a door sound is heard)

Imagery of the mind

Chorus

Could this be love?
Could this be illusion?
I'm I loosing my entire mind
Could this be lust?
Do I call it?
An imagery of the mind
(repeat Chorus)

Verse 1

I keep holding you crazy
Lingering in my mind
I see you in my dream
As you talk and hold my hands
I know you are with him, but I can't understand
why my heart keeps yelling over all for you.
Repeat chorus

Verse 2

Could I be crazy?
I'm losing my mind
Something says deep inside me
You are the one that I will say
Will you be my love my one.
I have this feeling
lingering inside me.

Sing to me my bird

Verse one

What wrong with you (oh . . . .)
My lovely bird
Quiet as never you stare at me (yeah yeah)
You don't sing to me anymore (not anymore . . . .)
Bik . . . Bik . . . Bik . . . Bik . . . Bik
That's how you use to (yeah as you use to)
Sing to me oh my bird please

CHORUS

Maybe you have something in your mind my bird
I love you more my little bird
I'm like a butterfly attracted more and more
to a flower even when the color is subtle
oh . . . . sing to me my bird

VERSE two

Are you sad tell me ? I will make you smile
Are you tired? let me know your mind?
Are you in pain? I'm here to help
Are you in love? then sent me to pains
I will do it all because I love you
Don't be silent my lovely bird
I need to hear your voice
(Repeat chorus till it fades

I don't want to be that girl anymore

Verse one

Don't Say you're sorry, because you are not
Don't say you need me back, because you are bluffing
Don't say you regret, because you have said it before
Don't tell me I'm changed, because you cannot be spotless
Don't tell me "You belong with me" because that's an old story"
Before my eyes you say I'm your princess
Before your friends you say I'm a loser

[Chorus]

Let the tidal blow and the water watch away our love
From your shell I break of
From our past I strike away
From our memories I shy away
I'm not that girl you use to know (not anymore)
I'm changed . . . (changed for the better)
I have broken free from your chains
I'm not yours not anymore
I don't want to be that girl anymore

Verse 2

That girl which you sneak into her room
The girl you felt ashamed to be seen with
You grinned when she smiled
In your eyes, all you saw was her mistakes
She was incomparable to your flings

She was stupid because she loved you
Don't adore her anymore with lies but scorned with the heart
She doesn't want to be the same girl anymore

Bridge

But I break away from the past that had hold me
I cannot (I cannot) be the same girl tomorrow
I break off (break off) from that girl who was never saw her self
I'm not . . . . And can never be the same girl
I don't want to be the same girl not anymore

Chorus

Let the tidal blow and the water watch away our love
From your shell I break of
From our past I strike away
From our memories I shy away
I'm not that girl you use to know again (not anymore)
I'm changed . . . (changed for the better)
I have broken free from your chains
I'm not yours not anymore
I don't want to be that girl anymore

Outro

Let the shadow of the yesterday fade away
Let light replace the darkness
Let me smile to myself once more
With the wings of an eagle I fly
I will sow higher as my spirit takes me

Because I don't want to be that girl anymore
Don't close your eyes because it is real

No no, No, not me
Not that girl anymore . . . .
I cannot be
No . . . . not me
Don't close your for this real
Ya yeah yeah yeah ya
I'm leaving
Yea . . . . I don't want to be that girl anymore
More . . . . ooooooooo
I don't want be that girl anymore . . . .

Because of him

Casting
I see my body casted
To the floor as I chant
This words that flow in to my mind

Racing

Racing my heart skips as the memories race back
I know I can take it no more but can't erase it
from my past or the future.

Chorus

I know we had our difference
We cannot denied we are different beings
But one thing is sure our child can't face the differences
We can't get let him inherit our hindrance
So why don't we come back to be because of him . . . .
for he needs our love together . . . .
Huh . . . .

Pre chorus

Because of him . . . mmmmmmmm
We can make it work ohooooo ho ho . . .
Because of him.

Verse 2

Now I know
you are bragging I took care of him all alone
I can read your mind you are asking why did you leave
Are you now coming because you want to say oh daddy
I love him as my son so I want us to be together
Because of him . . . . mmmmmm

When you said you loved me
Where you ready to hold me?
Didn't you know it will be about him
It is not all about me but him
So I will say yes (say yes . . . .)
Hmmmmmm
Because of him

Chorus

I know we had our difference
We cannot denied we are different beings
But one thing is sure our child can't face the differences
We cant get let him inherit our hindrances
So why don't we come back to be because of him . . . .
For, he needs our love together . . . . Huh . . . .

Outro

Baby I promise (I . . . . promise)
To never let go(no no no no)
We will stay together
Have him together
Because of him . . . .
Uuhhhhhhhhhh uhhhhhhhh

You believed in me

Verse 1

Remember you last words
That someday I will be free
To sing out loud
Remember you smiling
You're telling me that I will scream
You will scream ho
Not ashamed of whom you are
I couldn't believe you, yet you believed in me
I couldn't have made it without you
Thanks for believing in me

Chorus

Because you believe in me
Hmmmm ye . . . .
I will cross the deep sea
Climb the mountain
For your strength is here in me
Because you believe in me . . . .

(Pre chorus)

Do you believe in me?
I know I m not strong
I need you to get strong do you believe in me
Believe in believe in . . . .
Do you believe in me?

Verse 2

In your dying bed
I kept your words lingering in my heart
Because I know you believe in me
Now as I sing out your words will never die
Because you believed in me
Flashback on yesterday around the fire just warming up
You tap my head and said to me, you will be hot like fire
I couldn't believe you, yet you believed in me
Today I can sing out and shout hora
Thanks for believing in me
(repeat chorus)

Outro

Hulahla hulahalala . . . .
Hulalahulalalala . . . .
Thank you grandmum
You are so great . . .
For believing in me
I never thought that I will sing this but by your strength
Hulalahulala . . . .

Dance with me

Intro

Beats . . . .
Instrumentals
My heart skips
Instrumentals

Verse 1

Baby I' m staring at just you
You imagine how my heart just flows
Your steps makes my heart go slow (I need . . . . you steps)
To make it fast
Your dashing beauty makes me smile, could you please give me your hands to
the beat of the rhythm
Let that body come rob on me let me feel your sensational music.

Chorus

Baby will you dance with me
This is all I need
I m not asking for something had for you
All I need is your twisted waist
Which will bring the power out of me?
Will you give me just those steps?
Baby, will you dance with me

Verse two

Step down to the dance floor
Let me see what you have for me
I can see in your eyes it says more
Come along just make me scream
I can feel your sexy arms
It makes my heart to go in flames

Bridge

hu hu hu
mmmmm
hmmmmmm
Roll it for me
You are sexy
so so hmmm amazing
Keep rocking keep rocking
Baby rock my world

Outro

wo ooh . . . .
A pretty girl like you makes me dashing
Here comes my joy coming so flashing
hooo . . . . ho
Pretty girls like you are so rare
What you do makes my world go crashing
Dance with me dance with me dance with me ho . . . ho . . . hu ho hu
Come rock me come rock me come rock me . . . . you are so dashy

What's on your mind?

Intro

A and b

Could you tell me . . . . ?
Tell me . . . .
Tell me what's on your mind
mmmmmmmmmmm
Because I'm thinking . . . .
Have you had it for so long?

Verse 1

B

Ho yeah . . . .
I remember the first time I set my eyes on you
When I said hi
And you say hey the words came down my mind

A

You remind me of that very day
When you walked up to my side
I was sighing
Although seeing, the e beauty the world had beneath

Chorus

A and B

And you said hey . . . .
And my heart raced . . . .
I began feeling so different than I had ever been
And I knew at that moment you are my missing self
I said I can never let go
(Repeat chorus)

Verse 2

A

And then you came in to me without backing out at all
And I gave you my love without saying no
And till this moment . . . which I m standing afar I can't regret that special
moment of the day we met . . . of the day we met . . .

B

I still keep on holding unto that special kiss
That you placed you lips to my lonely one
And gave me the strength to breath and live again
Though you not with me, I can't just let it go

(Repeat chorus)

Bridge

Will we keep on . . . ? (Echo) keep on . . . .
Holding onto the past
But we keep on keep on moving on with our life
I'm hurting (Echo) hurting deep inside
It keeps reminding me, oh . . . here in my heart . . . .

So tell me, why did you have to go?
To someone who will you tear us apart?
Why did you have to leave to?
The one who you make us two

(Repeat chorus)

Beautifull liar

Intro

I wish I could fly, fly way
to a place where the is no you
You tell me believe in me because
I will always love you, but I see that we been a fairy tale

Verse 1

Why do you lie
When you know it doesn't pay
You rip my hear whenever you lie
Why do you lie when all it pays is pain?
do you want to be a beautiful liar?

Chorus

A beautiful liar doesn't fit you at all
It makes you stink to me
A beautiful liar doesn't fit you all
It makes me want to cry
Say the truth and be free from the chain
Of being . . . . a beautiful liar.

verse 2

You tell me she is your sister
Always playing with my heart
Do you like her, do you prefer her most

Missing you

Verse 1

As the river stood still
I knew my life without you was dormant
A lonely heart of me, who will it belong?
For words alone can't convey my feelings
my heart needs you so more and more
ohhhhhhhhhhhh ohh . . . .

Chorus

I missed you lot, oh my baby
Though you be mile away
You are in my heart
It will always meet in the lightening
which will sparkle my heart to need you more and more.

Verse 2

The space between us makes me go hissing
I need you baby, I feel like kissing you.
I need you and I'm missing
I remember you and all you're teasing
My heart can't be leasing, it still belong to you
Your lovely eyes gladdens my heart

(repeat chorus)

Secretly admiring

Intro

Tell me . . . .
What do you think of me?
Do you love me too?
Don't say you don't see the sparkles that rise in my eyes . . . .

Verse 1

Every time I wait on the bus
All I need is you coming around
When I sleep all I need is
Seeing you beautiful smile
Your beautiful smile gives me shelter
Without your love I will go crazy.
Without you there is no day or night.
What will I do without you?
Baby baby baby i need you
I want spend my life, all with you

Chorus

Secretly admiring . . . .
All the day admiring . . . .
I wish I could curdle through the night . . . .
Oh oh . . . Secretly admiring . . . .
Wising to be in you arms . . . .

Baby please don't say . . . .
Don't say . . . .
You don't see the sparkles in my eyes

(repeat chorus)

Verse 2

Baby I need you . . .
I need you to high on me . . . .
I m so lonely
Lonely without you
You are so homely,
My type of woman
Come touch slowly
Get soft on me
I will go so deeply
Deeply in love with you

(Repeat xrus)

I'm Risen

Verse 1

A

The darkness keeps shading away
My grieving keep fading away
My stopped heart starts skipping
While my past keep sinking
I feel I'm not falling
I'm rising . . . .

B

My pouring tears are drying
My love says keeps driving
My fallen heart stops breaking
The memories stops lingering
I'm rising . . . .

Chorus

You are the reason . . . .
That my heart can move again
You are the reason . . . .
That my voice can say it loud
You are my reason . . . .

I can shout out loud . . . .
I'm risen . . . . uhhhhhhhhh because of you . . . .

Verse 2

A

I can recall, the last the day the sun shone on me
For I had been hiding and crying in my room
Asking myself . . . . why . . . did love have to die
We thought we will make it.
Until death stroke, it took my love way. Never to smile or sing again until that
great day, you shone your smile at me
And now I can sing, shout it loud . . . ohh . . . .
You are the reason . . . .

B

Its been a decade since I smile
Since the day that love crashed my heart
I stop breathing, stop loving
But hated life
But you came by, passing around my window
and your shadow spoke to me out loud
You better rise up, for you are alive again.
And now I sing . . . .

repeat xrus

Bridge

The power of your love has made me rise
Since the moment your ray shone to my life
I had been speechless
I had been motionless
But the power of your love made me rise
repeat xrus

Betrayed by love

Verse 1

A

That yesterday, I caught you in his bed
it's like today, so lingering in my heart
I can feel the pain
as you stoke you hands on his back
It keep piecing down my heart.
I have been betrayed, betrayed by my love

B

I never wanted
but he took me into it
I said I loved you but he said forget about him
and when he kissed . . . . me . . . .
The touch to my lips kindled
You never did. hmmmm what he did to me . . . hmmm, never before.

Chorus

I can feel that pain as it strokes down my heart
Can you feel pain, I don't think you did
For all you do is laugh and hurt the ones you love
It isn't fun . . . . don't do that no anymore
It isn't fun to me even to them the ones you smile at their hurt

Favor U

Verse 1

A

So you now telling me, what it feels like to be with him
I can't believe this, you don't care at all
What do you think that the heart is just a doll?
Do you have feelings at all . . . .
I don't need you no more . . . .
I can't take you any more . . . .
You are so heartless, so stay away from me
I don't need you . . . . uhooo
I don't want to be betrayed by love uuhhh not anymore

B

It's new . . . . like I happened yesterday
The feelings from his finger, u can't tell
I never said I needed you back
So you watch what you say to me
All I said just give me a chance
Let me show you . . . Show you . . . what he did to me . . . .
Because you pretended . . . . like you never knew it before . . . .

Chorus

I can feel that pain as it strokes down my heart
Can you feel pain, I don't think you did
For all you do is laugh and hurt the ones you love
It isn't fun . . . . don't do that no anymore
It isn't fun to me even to them the ones you smile at their hurt.

Are you the one

Intro

Tanatan . . . . tan . . . . tan . . . . tainniiin . . . .

Verse one

Oh I sing
You are smiling me
From our far you look at me
Can you hear?
Can you heal me?
From this broken heart from one

Chorus

For all I need is a friend
Someone who cares
I need a shoulder to cry on when tears drip my eyes
Are you that someone that I need?
I need someone today.

Verse 2

Oh I loved
Now I know you are one for me
Could you love me more than he ever did?
Oh I need that love one
Will you be the one I need for me?

Bridge

And can carry me
I need . . . . a love . . . .
Someone . . . . Who will love . . . .
Please be . . . . My love . . . .
For all I need is a friend
Please be that friend

I'm a woman of worth

Intro

On my hair will they be a crown
if see this
I believe it
I dream it
I will achieve it
Nothing will stop me from making it
i . . . m (echo) yes i . . . m.
A woman (woman). Woman of worth.

Verse 1

Looking into the mirror, who do I see?
A potential statue of beauty
An adornment of great strength
To her feet, they stride in honor
Walking down the aisle in royal apparel of purple linen
In awe they look up with their eyes popping out from their sockets in golden blue
To the throne, they lay her heart to merry
A goddess on earth, a magnifying creation from Mother Nature

Bridge

The thought I won't make it
but on . . . they lied
The mirror girl is now me
My fairy tales do come true

Chorus

I don't care or give a damn
About what the world might say
neither do I care about, who the eyes might see
For I' m a woman . . . . a woman . . . . a woman of worth

Verse 2

To my feet I will stride gracefully
And the world will be astound
My friends and family will say
So Cinderella story still come true
The old me will be a thing of the past
My past will now be the girl in the mirror
And my dreams will be my true life
I believe yeah I do, I' m a woman of worth

Bridge

The thought I won't make it
but oh . . . they lied
The mirror girl is now me
My fairy tales do come true

Chorus

I don't care or give a damn
about what the world might say
neither do I care about, who the eyes might see
For I' m a woman . . . . a woman . . . . a woman of worth

I miss you

(INSTRUMENTATION)

oooooooo
ummmmmm

Verse 1

ooooooo
Oh my love I'm missing
My heart here keeps racing
Memories keep flashing
On that day you were leaving
Here on my bed I'm asking
Why did you have to leave me?
Here with a lonely heart
I cry and ask why . . . why . . . why . . . why . . . why

Chorus

Why did you go
I miss you, oh my baby
Is like waiting on years without you
My love for you is endless
My life without you is meaningless
Tell me why oh ba . . . by because I miss you

Verse 2

hmmmmmmmmmmm
Under the rain I can feel its droplet down on my skin
The water keeps drenching down my skin
My skin gets dry, my body is thirsty
This makes me yield more and more for you
I miss you . . . .
One thing I know is that our heart belongs
but I can't predict if you will change your mind someday
I promise I will be waiting for you

Chorus

Why did you go?
I miss you, oh my baby
Is like waiting on years without you
My love for you is endless
My life without you is meaningless
Tell me why oh ba . . . by because I miss you
I miss you my love

I'm sad that I let you go
Even though I try to be strong
Saying you isn't a part of me
No matter how hard I try
To keep my mind waving away from you

Blessed one

Intro

A
Call me blessed
B
For I just found a blessed one
Both
I love you blessed one (echo) blessesd one blessed one

Verse 1

A
Touch me (echo) I' m the most blessed
B
Hold me (echo) i m the most blessed
A
Let the river of your love wash my tears away
B
Let the strength of your love make me strong
Both
Your love is so supernatural

Chorus

Your super being makes me smile
You are unique love makes me want to shed tears of joy
Your rare creation makes me say,
I' m the most blessed

Verse 2

A
Closely (echo) come nearer, blessed one
B
Lovely (echo) the radiant of your eyes makes me smile
A
Whisper into my awaiting eyes
B
Say those words I have been waiting to hear blessed ones
Both
The phenomenon of your love dazzles me

Chorus

Your super being makes me smile
You are unique love makes me want to shed tears of joy
Your rare creation makes me say,
I'm the most blessed

Bridge

Say to me oh my blessed one
Happy I found . . . . you (Echo)
So blessed one give me more love
I love you from the beginning till the ends of the earth
I'm the blessed one.

Chorus

Your super being makes me smile
You are unique love makes me want to shed tears of joy
Your rare creation makes me say,
'I' m the most blessed

My boo

Chorus

Say it right
Stand upright
I write you down my boo

Verse 1

They have been talking to me and teasing
Why do you go around with this placard
She is not fit to be your woman
But I got something to say to them
I write you down my boo

Chorus

Say it right
Stand upright
I write you down my boo

Verse 2

I'm not ashamed of you (not at all)
Even though you don't go into class
I bet my life might go into slashes
If our love go though crashes
But I write you down my boo

Chorus

Say it right
Stand upright
I write you down my boo

Brigde

Girl I know we have been fighting
Thinking that I have been cheating
And they all have been talking
I want us to make things right (echo) things right . . . .
For I write you down my boo

Chorus

Say it right
Stand upright
I write you down my boo

Outro

My boo . . . . boo boo boo boo
my boo boo boo boo boo boo . . . .
I write you down my boo
You are my cherish woman
My one and all so cherished
I write you down my boo
Hu . . . .

Story of a sour love

Intro

(instrumental)

Verse 1

Here on the river side
I recall clearly the flow of blood from my battered hands
Mum said she couldn't take it no more
Dad said he was sick of her
I could hear sounds of battering on chairs
I Hide behind the door and watched them fight about a sour love
I coudnt bear the word goodbye

Chorus

Because it ripped my heart apart
Thought of loosing you eluded my mind
I thought I could do better
So I made a mistake that coudnt be undone.

Verse 2

Years latter dad and mum, became me
The only one I thought had given me love was about leaving
I just returned from correction centre a year ago
Because of a past mistake

I thought my life won't be the same anymore
She was pushing me to do it again
I couldn't take the word goodbye (not at all)

Chorus

Because it ripped my heart apart
Thought of loosing you eludes my mind
I thought I could do better
So I made a mistake that couldn't be undone anymore

If I Had One More Chance

CHORUS

If i had . . . .
One more chance to live again in this world
I will make the one closer to smile again without a tickle . . . .
If only (if only) i could have another chance . . .
hu . . . .

Verse 1

And if . . . you were
to leave the world today?
What will you do to another life?
Will you smile, grin, laugh or cry?
Will you make them life to smile?
Will you kiss away the tears and sooth her pains?

CHORUS

if I had . . . .
One more chance to live again in this world
I will make the one closer to smile again without a tickle
if only (if only) I could have another chance . . .
hu . . . .

VERSE 2

Was born into the world to be a blessing
a touching hands to all, but I fled my mission
till death came around and took me away
now I wish everyday . . . .
that I could turn back the hands of time
then I will be a philanthropist and do my best.

CHORUS

if i had . . . .
One more chance to live again in this world
I will make the one closer to smile again without a lickle
if only (if only) I could have another chance . . .
hu . . . .

Bridge

Lot of people in the world are dying, from hunger, drought, earthquake
What do you do to help them?
Are you a supporting hands or an undertaker?
please just rise up and help the needy ones

don't be wishing or procrastinating
or be like the old me, who was greedy and selfish
he thought only about himself
there might be no tomorrow . . . .
you have just one more chance, so take the spear
because . . . .

Favor U

Chorus

if i had . . . .
One more chance to live again in this world
I will make the one closer to smile again without a tickle
if only (if only) I could have another chance . . .
hu . . . .

Shout hey . . . ho . . .

Verse 1

Look through the mirror
Who do you see
That's a true reflection
Of who you truly are

Chorus

So shout hey . . . .ho . . . .
Don't be afraid to let it out
Let your light shine bright
To the people who you love

Repeat chorus

Verse 2

That's you who's smiling
Just at me
Its an imagination
(Gasp) oh my fantasy

Chorus

Bridge

I say hey . . . hey . . . hey . . . hey . . . hey . . . hey . . . .
Ho . . . ho . . . . ho . . . ho . . . ho . . . . ho . . . . ho . . . ho . . . .

To the people who you love
Repeat 2times before chorus

Chorus

So shout hey . . . . ho . . . .
Don't be afraid to let it out
Let your light shine bright
To the people who you love

POEMS

Tears of joy

Tears of joy

Streams down my chin as I look at her innocent face

I hold her in my arms and feel great comfort

My heart leaps for joy as my baby is born

Born to the world to be more than a friend to me

Thought of guilt

Thought of guilt stream my mind

The event waves in my head

I feel like going crazy

I'm disturbed by thought of guilt in me.

It keeps ringing loudly in my mind

I'm a victim of the my guilt.

My sensational taboo

Pour your wine to a lonely vessel of honor.

Touch my skin so softly, that I crave so hot for it.

Whisper to my ears so lovely

Make me go crazy and hail wild.

Breathe me in you, along the liquor of my breath.

To my sense crawl your finger thoroughly.

Make me yell, I love you a million times.

But remember

No matter what you do, you will always be my sensational taboo.

Hallucination

Who are they?

Hiding in spotlight yellow rays?

Behind green leaves they veil their shades

Down to earth to destroy,

I believe to the fate of man will be kill or die

Their appearance is masked with terror

oh ooooooo a slight pain in me

My crackle head makes me know

I'm sick, for they are all imaginary figure

I'm only hallucinating.

Oh your face

Veil away the cloudy horizon that prevents me from seeing your face

Oh that face, that lovely face you remind me

That face that use to smile or wink at me in my neighborhood

Till a stranger came and swept her away

to a place I would see her no more

Oh that face, that lovely face you remind me.

I need an angel

I need an angel

Someone who I could call my friend

Someone who will wipe my tears

Someone who will stand by me when I need help

Someone I can say a friend in need is a friend indeed

All I need is an angel

Mirage in a maids mind

A dream of you and me in deep comfort

dancing around the fountain singing love songs

In both arms we swirl around in joy

Oh my king and his maid are in love.

So filled with joy till I awaken from my dream

Clean my shoe, make my tea and do the chores

I wish my dream was the latter

I'm alive

Side by side we lay
Sound of romance fills the air
with our bodies rob together
Your love has made me alive.

I miss you

Thoughts of you eludes my mind

like a fish without water I might die

Your space is vacuum occupied by dust of memories.

Every time the wind blows, it takes it away

but like a mighty ocean you fill my thought again

my endless love, why did you go?

I wish I saw it coming

I would have stopped death from taking you away

I miss you my love, I miss you

Pretty one

Like the power of the mighty ocean you swift my breath away

Your charming glamour is what I can't resist

You are a seed of the peach tree in Eden

A true beauty of the fruit of loom

Oh pretty one, say you are mine.

Far and away

On waves of wind I stand

staring into the space.

Thinking about my rips and the distance between us

Softly in my ears I can hear her say

Though we are far away

You are here in my hearts

See you soon my love.

Scared of your love

Tears drips down my face

My heart keeps racing

I cant breath anymore.

You are an emotional pain

that pierce though my skin

I m scared of your love.

Age of innocence

The age of innocence was washed away by the flood of Noah

The unborn light have been slain by magical fusion

An age of superstition remains

An age of confusion, is where I exist

With it, mystery unfolds as the day rolls by

An age where the unknown is leant before birth

An age which our first speech are centralized

On never polished but obscene sounds

I'm a creature of an age of impurity

An age of strive for survival

A beautiful woman

Woman of substance
with inspiring beauty
I'm a beautiful woman

A lily in the mist of blossoming flowers
A beauty so vivid in the mist of others
I'm a beautiful woman

When I step the board
They step a bound
around me majestically the fall
For I m a beautiful woman

My flawless motion
makes them motionless
To me they are my admirers
For I'm a beautiful woman

In awe they will hold me
To my skin like flies to red meat
I won't be held to awe
For I m a beautiful woman

The heart that once loved me

I'm back to the arms of the one I once love

I had wondered away from him

Thinking the world out there had a lot for me

but there I met empty promise and deceit

then I knew the heart that once loved me

was waiting for me.

What is Love

What do you say is love?

Some say love is a calm river that turns wild in distress

Some say it is pure water that calms the soul

To me love is an under estimated feelings

A passion that rises between two beings

A phenomenal power that quenches fire

If you say love is strong

That's an understatement

Love is just a word, but the feelings remains unexpressed in word

Tides with strong powers in between two hearts

Bonds lot of people as one no matter their difference

A feelings with phenomenal powers

That is love.

Color of emotion

We hurt the ones who love us without remorse

Even when we are caught in the act we deny

With our kinds we mingle and receive words of praise

We take our lovers heart for a game chart

Color of emotion is all we need

It was meant to be

Now I know why the bird sings

The tree blows

The river grows tidal

The flowers sprangle with beauty

Why I admire the beauty of nature

Why my heart beats for you

It was meant to be

I can't fight against your love

I'm sad that I let you go

Even though I tried to be strong

Saying you are not a part of me

No matter how hard I tried

To keep my mind waving away from thought of you

I feel strong bubble of tears, as they hit my eyes to swell

Down to my feet they stretch like a river of tears I cry

In my memory it rubbles

I can't fight against your love

Feelings

Feeling of pain overwhelms me

Feelings of sadness lay in my heart

Feelings of Loneliness evolves all around me

I bent myself to the floor and cry alone

Feelings of rejection is all I sing

Broken heart

Why does the ones we love hurt us bad

Like a door blown a jar by the wind

It tears our hearts to shamble

It causes endless tears to drip to our feet

So we lay our heart ashore

Waiting for a warm river to sooth our pain

Wash away our pain

And when the ever waited river comes

It washes awhile and leaves our hearts broken again.

Adieu my love

Now that you are gone
I m pondering in the sun
setting my hearts on the lost me and you
you are gone away, I m now so left alone
wailing in pain and watching away
the steps you left in my heart
adieu my love.

oh my love, I wish

I wish I can turn back the hands of time

I wish I could put back the pieces

I wish we could swivel once again

I wish our backs could be laid once more

on the sand of the beach

with our hands wrapped in each other embrace

we will lay on it and watch the evening stars

I wish our life could be back again

oh my love, I wish.

I await your love

To my open arm, I await your love

Side by side we will lay the ocean

In bare our feelings shall grow strong emotion

Lyrics from the wave shall lead our motion

Then, the rising sun will be gone low

Touch my skin softly that I crave more

Pour your wine to my vessel of honor

Whisper to my ears, make me go wild

Like a snake crawl on my sense mildly

Make me scream "I love you" so wildly

To me will the veil of honor belong?

Like river your love will flow my vein

Of the finest angels you have chosen me

A mother bee stuck on your honey skin

All for me you scorn them in sin

Under the blue evening stars we shall twin

Like clove of garlic we shall stick together
The river tides shall be glad for us
Birds of the season shall spread our tales
The sea horizon shall praise our love

When your sensational arms shall wrap around me
My heart shall affirmed my conquer in love
"let the river not wash away your footstep"
For it's a mark in my heart alone.

Here we are

Here we are

Moving side by side

Amidst the breeze

Flowing through the hemp of our garment

They said we won't make it

But now we sing a loud

We have made it even stronger than the hovering eyes

Which mocked and stared at our lonely hearts?

Secrets

A garden of mischief
Needs more than tender from
the nurturing arms of a mother
Watered to keep it going
Day after day un-revealed.

My mother once told me a story
Never tell a secret
but with all the needle the world has
Sew it sealed from air.

I have grown with these words
To never tell a secret
But water and tender it
to grow in my heart alone.

The color of love

Who said the color of love is white

Who painted it black anyway?

Freely given by nature

Not to be withheld by man

But shared abundantly from the deepest of our heart

Feelings shared without any bond or attachment

Feelings that overlooks every pigment or infirmity

Its color is as innocent as ram

The color of love I know, is colorless.